To: ....

From: ....

Date: ....

A note to Mom

with love . . .

I love you, Mom!

Cherished word gifts from my heart to yours

Blythe Daniel & Helen McIntosh

Tyndale House Publishers
Carol Stream, Illinois

LIVING EXPRESSIONS
COLLECTION

Living Expressions invites you to explore God's Word in a way that is refreshing to your spirit and restorative to your soul.

Visit Tyndale online at tyndale.com.

Visit the author online at theblythedanielagency.com.

Tyndale, Tyndale's quill logo, *Living Expressions*, and the Living Expressions logo are registered trademarks of Tyndale House Ministries.

I Love You, Mom! Cherished Word Gifts from My Heart to Yours

Designed by Jacqueline L. Nuñez

For information about special discounts for bulk purchases, please contact Tyndale House Publishers at csresponse@tyndale.com, or call 1-855-277-9400.

ISBN 978-1-4964-5257-3

Printed in China

28	27	26	25	24	23	22
7	6	5	4	3	2	1

Honor her for all that her hands have done, and let her works bring her praise at the city gate.

PROVERBS 31:31, NIV

The Gift of You

Hello, Mom!

You have just opened a gift for dear you because *you* are a gift! You are so loved! Inside these pages you are celebrated for being an amazing mom to your family and for the many ways your hard work and care make a difference each day.

God chose you to be a mom. That's a gift you have unwrapped! He has always known the dynamics of your family and how you would play an important role in shaping your child from his or her early years through adulthood.

As a mother-and-daughter team, we know that sharing a sentiment can be a great way to show that you are on your child's heart. This book contains more thoughts than a greeting card. It takes many pages to express the love and thanks for what you have meant to your family. Not a single card could cover that successfully. We hope the sentiments will help you recall the ways you are seen and appreciated for the many contributions you bring to your child's life.

The devotions are designed to express love and thanks through word gifts that are meant to lift your heart when

you need them the most. Perhaps your child has given you homemade gifts over the years that grace your home. Now your child is giving you words meant to grace your heart!

We hope you feel joy rising in you when you think of how much you are loved and that your heart is filled with thanks for how God brought you and your child together. You are honored as someone who gives out so much love and deserves so much in return.

> Listen to your father, who gave you life,
>   and don't despise your mother when she is old.
> Get the truth and never sell it;
>   also get wisdom, discipline, and good judgment.
> The father of godly children has cause for joy.
>   What a pleasure to have children who are wise.
> So give your father and mother joy!
>   May she who gave you birth be happy.

PROVERBS 23:22-25

We believe your child wants you to be happy and to smile with joy as you read this book. It offers words from their heart that you can hold on to for a lifetime. May the gifts inside encourage you! It is with great pleasure that we invite your child to say, "I Love You, Mom!"

Blythe Daniel
Helen McIntosh

Holding Treasure Close

[Jesus] went down to Nazareth with them and was obedient to them. But his mother treasured all these things in her heart.

LUKE 2:51, NIV

Don't you love it when everything lines up just as you had hoped in a given day, without deviating from the plan? There is a semblance of safety that drops down like an oxygen mask in an airplane when you can see what's in front of you and plan for what's ahead. But when things don't go according to plan, you have to retrace your steps—and your hopes.

Have you thought about how Mary, the mother of Jesus, felt when she could not find her twelve-year-old son? Talk about the need for an oxygen mask! She and Joseph were on their way from Jerusalem back to Nazareth with a group of travelers when they realized he was missing. Retracing their steps, they frantically searched for him until they found him three days later in the Temple courts. The son that Mary wanted within arm's reach was in a place they likely didn't expect, interacting with those who were shaping the religious beliefs and practices of the day. And he was only twelve.

No doubt a celebration took place after Mary and Joseph found Jesus, which must have felt like a complete relief to Mary, who had carried him in her heart since conception. But she questioned Jesus, asking him how he could have treated them like that. Jesus said, "Why did you need to search? . . . Didn't you know that I must be in my Father's house?" (Luke 2:49).

Later we see that Mary, the mother of this young man who had a strength about him and a desire to love his Father, held these things in her heart. She recognized the treasure her son was and wanted to hold on to this treasure tightly. But she also recognized the one whom she was raising was a delight to God.

Sometimes as mothers we get caught up in the chase and don't think about the lives we are helping to mold. We often feel we can't hold our child close enough or long enough. Maybe, like Mary, you have thought about how you can hold on to the treasure of time and not release your child to the world just yet. You want to know that the one you are raising is close by.

Do you recognize the gift of loving your son or daughter, who needs the love only you can provide? We need to express our love even on the days that don't go as planned. Like Mary, we don't get to hold on to our treasure forever, but the treasure is still in our hearts. And so is the one you love.

you are . . .

a treasure

Mom, I know you say treasure is something you have, not what you look for. I am grateful to you for always making me feel like I am a treasure to you. You have lovingly taught me to find value in others and to care for my family and friends. I thank you for holding out the treasure of a mother's love for me. Thank you for finding me and caring for me when I have strayed from you and your heart for me. I treasure you in my heart as well.

Looking Back

Every time I think of you, I give thanks to my God.

PHILIPPIANS 1:3

Do you remember waving to your son or daughter in your pajamas as they boarded the school bus? Or watching them walk through the school doors until they were out of sight, wishing you could have said just one more thing to make sure they knew you didn't mean to be short with them at breakfast?

You wonder, *Will they remember those words or that tone more than the deeper values I have shared with them? Will they remember my outbursts or the "I wish I hadn't said that" moments more than the times I applauded them, noticed them, sought them out before bed, or comforted them after the game that didn't turn out so well?*

As moms, we hope our children will always remember our love for them more than our impatience or anger. We look back at the years we kept after them, repeating "I love you," trying to impress the words on their hearts and minds. And as the years progress, we want to tell them, "Every time I think of you, I give thanks for you."

It's easy to love our children when they're all snuggled up or have made it home before curfew or have called even when they didn't have to. And sometimes we think that if we can just get a few more uplifting words in, they'll remember those moments more than the times we lost it—when our tongues got tangled up with our minds and made a mess of our words—or the times we didn't say a word and our silence met with their stare.

No matter the situation, we can take great relief knowing that even when we fail, when our love has taken a back seat to our exhaustion and irritability, God loves our children perfectly—and he models that love for us so we can love our children better each day. We can ask for his patience, strength, and humility to seek forgiveness from our children when we need a fresh start. And we can be assured that God's love multiplies. He helps us add on layers of love to our children's lives when we voice how thankful we are for them and how they are help-ing us see his love through them. In this way our families experience how God's love always expands.

you are . . .

thankful

Mom, you have always said you are thankful to God for me, but I am the one who wants to say that I'm thankful for you. I remember how you cheered me on and helped me realize I really could solve a problem on my own. I have learned to be a better person because of you. If it were not for the ways you loved us within our home, I couldn't have learned to love as well outside our home. You have been the one who has always stood by my side and the one I still come home to. When I think of you, Mom, I give thanks to God.

Love Increasing

May the Lord make your love for one another and for all people grow and overflow, just as our love for you overflows.

1 THESSALONIANS 3:12

Remember the day when you first held your child and thought, *There is not enough room in my heart to hold all this love. I may burst with joy!* You had no idea then just how that love could find its cozy place in your life and how much it would grow. From the newborn days to the teenage years, you've shaken off sleep, stepped out of a warm bath, and dropped everything to make sure your child has what they need. And out of your unconditional, increasing love, you are passing on a love that overflows.

Have you ever considered that if you look at the word *mom* upside down it spells *wow*? The wow of your love is seen and felt and overflowing from your heart. Maybe when your child was young, you taped a measuring stick to the wall, marking their height each passing year until he or she towers over you. Whatever you measure love by, you can know that you have made your mark—from feeding and taking care of your family's daily needs to watching your child grow and become a loyal, honest, and humble young person ready to take on the challenges of an adult. This love will help them as they come up against a world that may try to tear them down just as easily as you've tried to build them up.

What children need is love, and moms sure provide that in abundance. The world can try to divide us against each other, but the ways we hand out love—through our smiles, homemade treats, or hugs that wrap tightly like a blanket—are how we can help restore and increase the love in our children.

When we ask God to increase our love for our family, we are coming close to our heavenly Father's ways of the heart. Love abounding is his specialty—not love manufactured with human effort and striving, but boundless, selfless, unconditional love that doesn't have an ending point. Now, if only our energy levels could keep up as we love on our children!

you are . . .

abundant

Thank you for the abundant, unconditional love that you show me. I can look back and see numerous ways you chose to love me, even when I didn't deserve it. In the same way, I choose to love you unconditionally, abundantly, and in ever-increasing ways. Beyond my human capacity to love, I want God's love living in me. I can't love you like you deserve, but I know that he can give me his love for you.

God with You

Don't be afraid, for I am with you.
   Don't be discouraged, for I am your
    God.
I will strengthen you and help you.
   I will hold you up with my victorious
    right hand.

ISAIAH 41:10

Remember zipping across the street on your bike with streamers on the handlebars and a bell that signaled you were coming? Or laughing at how you got away with eating more cookie dough than your mom allowed? Or having friends over and enjoying time together with some late-night popcorn?

Now fast-forward to the life you have as a mom. Wouldn't it be great to go back to "the good old days" when your heart wasn't concerned about grown-up problems or being responsible for others or filled with anxiety that runs on autopilot? You wonder how you can comfort and calm your own child through their troubles when you need a little calming miracle yourself. In fact, in these moments, you throw up your hands and ask God for just that.

If anyone understood their need for God to be with them, it was Naomi and her daughter-in-law Ruth, who had lost their husbands and were traveling alone toward Judah. Can you imagine their worry? Naomi had told Ruth to go back to her homeland, Moab, and start again, but Ruth refused, saying, "Where you go I will go, and where you stay I will stay. Your people will be my people and your God my God" (Ruth 1:16, NIV). We can imagine that the young, heart-strong Ruth told an older Naomi, "You and I are more capable than we imagine. God will provide for us. We will stay together, and God will be with us."

Isn't that just what the young do? They help us see the brighter side of life. And don't we see that in our own kids? They remind us of, well, us. Speeding down the street on makeshift skates. Staying out just a bit longer to enjoy the fireflies. Pointing to the stars and thinking that God must be pretty big to paint such a magnificent sky.

The story of Ruth and Naomi is a really good reminder not to fear the future but to trust in God's plan. Fear could have crept into their relationship and cast a shadow on the road they would walk together, but they chose to trust God's daily provision for them. They didn't anxiously look too far into the future but experienced God with them and the grace he had for them each day.

In the same way, we can help ourselves and our children know that it's going to be okay when we're scared, when we need to make big decisions. We can assure them that when their footing isn't firm, they have a big and capable God who is with them wherever they go, and our hearts and prayers are with them too.

you are . . .

fearless

Mom, we both face challenges, but we can remind each other to be brave. We can choose to be full of faith in our days ahead rather than fearful. Thank you for always encouraging me through challenges and difficulty. You have left a lasting impression on me to live fearlessly and trust in God. In him we have strength for the days ahead. I love you, Mom!

Lost and Found

Each time he said, "My grace is all you need. My power works best in weakness." So now I am glad to boast about my weaknesses, so that the power of Christ can work through me.

2 CORINTHIANS 12:9

How many times have you spent hours turning your house upside down trying to find something that was lost? As mothers we are responsible for so many things, and when we lose something we feel as though *we* are lost. We wonder how we could have misplaced it.

The Bible tells a story of a woman who had ten silver coins but lost one. She turned on the light, cleaned her house, and searched until she found it. She was so delighted when she found the coin that she called her friends over to celebrate (Luke 15:8-10).

How many of us look within our own hearts when we feel lost, when we need to be reminded of what's worth finding there? If we could shine a flashlight into those places, what would we find? Some of us may be quick to look at what's on the outside and focus only on what others see—how we present ourselves, how put together we *seem*, how well we carry on a conversation, how on top of our game we are.

But looking within, we can be reminded of our true worth: The woman God delights in. The woman your children lean on. The woman who searches for what's missing in her heart and home until she finds it, even when it takes hard work.

Could it be that sometimes we need to lose something in order to remember that we aren't operating in our own strength? We can imagine the woman in the story fretting:

Where could I have put what was so valuable to me? Where is my confidence that I'll ever find it? Maybe we have tapped out all the strength we can muster and need to give our worries to God. Maybe we need to stop searching and say, "I need some help over here, God. Please come near."

We can live in confidence of his strength, not our own abilities. He is the One who celebrates when we look for him. He knows all along not just what we're missing but also where we need to rely on him. When we look within our hearts and turn toward God, our searching is never wasted.

You are . . .

confident

Mom, I see the confidence you carry even more than the load that stretches you. You are a beautiful example of capacity—that when God fills you, we receive what he's poured into you. The power of Christ is working through you. He says that his grace is all we need and that the power he gives is best seen in our weaknesses. May you see your weaknesses not as losses but as opportunities for his strength to shine in you!

"Do-Over"

I am about to do something new.
See, I have already begun! Do you
not see it?
I will make a pathway through the
wilderness.
I will create rivers in the dry
wasteland.

ISAIAH 43:19

Perhaps there are words and phrases you remember hearing from your child that you didn't think you'd hear again after your own childhood, but somehow your child picked up on them from friends. Or perhaps you remember when your child made a greeting card for someone but didn't like how it came out, or played a bad move on a board game, or had a squabble with a friend down the street. Whatever happened, you knew they needed a do-over.

As moms, we often find ourselves in the same situations. When our children say something that catches us off guard and we react in ways we regret, or when we share words we wish we could have kept from spilling out, we also seek do-overs.

There is glorious relief when we can say to our children (or to ourselves with humble hearts), "I need to start over. Will you start over with me?" The beauty of a do-over is that we can model to our children that it's okay to admit we need to start again. When many people mess up, they speak pridefully and try to persuade others to their side; but we can model humility and confess that we got it wrong.

The apostle Paul, when referring to becoming more like Christ, said in Philippians 3:13, "No, dear brothers and sisters, I have not achieved it, but I focus on this one thing: Forgetting the past and looking forward to what lies ahead." Paul realized that dwelling on his regrets and past mistakes led him nowhere, but keeping his eyes on the hope of Christ helped him to become more like Christ, who trusted his good Father's plan for his life. How might this look in your life? What regrets can you leave behind? What new paths of hope can you forge today?

When we start over and speak words of affirmation, encouragement, and humility, we become light in a dark world, especially to our children. Where we need to give words of hope and courage, we can leave a lasting impression of love. Let's let go of our mishaps and allow God to work in us anew each day so we can love our children well.

You are . . .

renewed

Mom, we can renew our relationship and choose to see each other in a new light. I want to work with you in areas where we can communicate more clearly. I am glad that we are honest with each other, and I love seeing God's refining work in both of us. I hope you see the many ways you light up my life!

Time for You

There is a time for everything,
*   and a season for every activity under*
*   the heavens:*
*   a time to be born and a time to die,*
*   a time to plant and a time to uproot . . .*
*   a time to weep and a time to laugh,*
*   a time to mourn and a time to dance.*

ECCLESIASTES 3:1-2, 4, NIV

Whoever came up with the phrase "Time flies" might not have been a mother. With needy children and endless responsibilities, the hours of the day (and night) can sometimes feel painfully slow.

But reflecting on years past often makes us take notice of our time. We can look back and see the way we kept the ship afloat, put together menu choices, washed and folded clothes, soaked up the smiles, and sopped up the tears that flowed as our babies, then toddlers, then teenagers shared their emotions with us. We realize there are times to laugh and times to weep with our children. Sometimes those moments erupt into dance or settle into a seriousness in which we see them through their struggles and show them we care.

If we were to fast-forward time through those long, slow days of early parenting, we might quickly realize how precious those early days were. Do you remember the first time you helped your child cross the street? Tie their shoes? Swing a bat? Or pedal a bike without training wheels?

The best gift you can give a child, teen, or young adult is your time. It's an investment you make, and you reap the benefits. When your toddler is frustrated, your time is what they need. When your teen doesn't understand how a friend could treat them in such a way, your listening ear is valuable. And when your child is grown and out on their own, you can look back at every moment spent, every memory made, and every lesson taught as something you gave them that can't be bought. It's genuine and lasts a lifetime.

The greatest part of time is that it has you in it. How are you using it? Do you give your finest to others and leave what's left to your children? Or do you see that the time you took to solve a problem, share advice when asked, and give words of approval has been worth it? Let's make it our goal that our families have our greatest time and focus. If one of the biggest needs of our children is to know they are loved, then let's show them through the gift of time.

you are . . .

attentive

Mom, when you give me your attention, I feel loved. Thank you for being attentive to my needs and for not putting aside what feels important to me. When you sit with me and give me your focus, it means you are letting other people, activities, and responsibilities wait. The time you spend with me is a gift and something I will not forget. Thank you for being such a wonderful listener. I want us to make as many memories together as we can.

A Gift for Generations

Let each generation tell its children of your mighty acts;
let them proclaim your power.

PSALM 145:4

"Which cookies are we making? The recipe that Grandma used for our birthdays?" With anticipation in their eyes, children love to figure out what treats are coming their way and whether they're ones from their sweet-filled memories. Passing down recipes is not only one way of carrying on family traditions but also a gift for generations to come. Some of the warmest memories fill our stomachs as well as our minds!

Other gifts we pass down include our hobbies, such as sewing or knitting those perfect sweaters or hats that get worn by one child and then another. Or we pass on what we know—allowing our children to take over responsibilities that previously were ours. By doing so, we show that we trust them and that there is a place for them to learn and grow.

God designed families to love each other and pass on his love from generation to generation. In fact, Psalm 100:5 says, "The LORD is good. His unfailing love continues forever, and his faithfulness continues to each generation." Even if you didn't receive the kind of love you deserved or hoped for as you were growing up, you have the opportunity to create traditions you want your children and grandchildren to carry into their years ahead. New traditions, habits, and attitudes can start with you. What would your designer's heart like to see happen? Who in your family would be able to help with this? Do you see what you are passing along to your loved ones?

There is a certain joy in seeing how God uses families to show the continuity of his love for us. One person shares with another or one generation serves the other, and before you know it, you are all sitting around the table giving thanks, being a part of a group of people that you call your own.

Know how much you play a vital role in shaping the younger generations. In the years to come, they will look back and say, "Mom/Grandmother was sure able to teach us a lot. What we do now is because of her."

Mom, your family is eager to hear from you. Are you ready to share your gifts and traditions?

you are . . .

a legacy

Mom, you are a legacy builder. Through your love, you have left a lasting mark on me, and I want to share that love with my own family. One of the beautiful things about sharing your wisdom and talents with me is that I have more of a window into your soul and what matters to you, like time spent with family and God. I won't lose sight of the legacy you have built and continue to build in my life. I want future generations to know the impact you've had on our family!

Forgiveness

Bear with each other and forgive one another if any of you has a grievance against someone. Forgive as the Lord forgave you.

COLOSSIANS 3:13, NIV

We don't often see *give* in the word *forgive*, do we? We forget that forgiveness is a gift—one we hope to receive when we have wronged others and one we can give away when others have wronged us.

But forgiveness is sometimes a difficult word to move from our mind to our lips. "Will you forgive me?" can feel like a mouthful, especially when mixed with our pride. Sometimes we think only of what another should say to us. But as mothers, we need to lead the way with our words.

There is a woman named Mary who, in recent years, lost her only son. As difficult as it was, she was overcome with the need to forgive the person who was responsible for her child's death. After some time, she was able to not only forgive this person but also help him upon his release from prison. She gave God the glory for her ability to forgive. She said her forgiveness wasn't just for him but for herself as well. She needed to release her bitterness in order to move ahead in her life. How touching to read her story and find out that the man she forgave ended up living right next door to her. Now that is a truly remarkable forgiveness story!

What would it take for you to forgive your child or ask their forgiveness for something you've held on to for far too long? Imagine the gift that releasing your burden could be to both of you. If there is anything standing in the way, take the hand of your child and put them first. When we enter the sacrificial role of raising our children, we need to lead the way in forgiveness. To give the gift of forgiveness and to receive it is the greatest opportunity to remember that as God has forgiven us, we are to forgive each other.

You are . . .

forgiven

Mom, I forgive you for anything you wish you could have done differently. I love you and want you to know how much I see you as one who is deserving of the very best in your life and in our relationship. I pray you can forgive me, too, for all the times I've hurt you. I always appreciate how you show me that you love me and welcome me back into your arms time and time again.

Choosing Joy

*Always be joyful. Never stop praying.
Be thankful in all circumstances, for
this is God's will for you who belong
to Christ Jesus.*

1 THESSALONIANS 5:16-18

Joy is like good cream in your coffee. It adds a splash of light and a beautiful design to what you are taking in. Joy warms you and is a smile your heart holds inside—not because everything is right in your life but because you've *chosen* to fill your spirit with it. You don't wait for joy to come knocking on your door but open your heart and home to it always.

Still, it's tough to be joyful in some of life's most difficult circumstances, isn't it? We can pretend everything is okay, but on the inside we are barely holding things together. Our joy is at the very bottom of the pile, weighed down by our loads. Sometimes these are literal loads—laundry bins stuffed to the brim, stacks of bills that need to be paid, heaps of leaves that need to be raked. The never-ending tasks of parenting and household chores can dampen our spirit if we let them.

The truth is, these responsibilities are just aspects of the deeper treasures of motherhood that lie beneath our sight at times. What a privilege and calling it is to be a mom and to bring life, hope, instruction, and encouragement to those whom God brings to our nest.

God tells us to always be joyful—and purposefully so. Even in the hard places, we must remember that we belong to Jesus and that through him we can trade our worries and anxiousness for joy. In doing so, we know

that the state of our spirit isn't based on what we see or feel but on a resolution and a way of life.

And we are modeling that joy for our children, which will help them to choose joy too. We can show them joy isn't something we decide to wear on a particular day, putting it on and taking it off if things don't go well. Rather, joy is a firm place in our hearts that flows through our mouths when we speak.

The spirit of joy is the center we go back to that no one can shake from us. It feels like the resting place we wish we could bottle up on vacation and take home with us. And we can—by inviting joy in and remembering that it is an outward expression of our inward hope in God.

you are . . .

joyful

Mom, you bring laughter into my life, and I appreciate how your joy is contagious. Your smile helps me
find my own, especially on days when I am weighed
down with life's problems and worries. I've watched
you choose joy in the hardest situations. Even when
it seemed impossible, you not only found joy but also
lived it. Seeing you make joy your mission helps me to
choose it also. I want to reflect that joy each day.

Serve It Up

God has given each of you a gift from his great variety of spiritual gifts. Use them well to serve one another.

1 PETER 4:10

"Dinner's ready—come and get it!" How often have you said this and suddenly the ones you call your children come bounding into the kitchen? Just moments before, they were in another part of the house, untouchable. But the delicious announcement of food drew them in like flies to a picnic!

Serving food is one of those things many moms do without overthinking it too much. But serving up generosity and a spirit that is willing to freely give to others? That is not as easy when we're running short on time, energy, patience, and a good number of other ingredients.

The disciple Peter shows us a better way. He served with Jesus on many occasions and recognized the many spiritual gifts that were in others. He even chose to leave behind his calling to show people who Jesus was and what he came to earth to do. He continually saw people's spiritual needs and led them to Jesus. Peter willingly and sacrificially served, loved, and healed others in Jesus' name.

We may not always serve with such purpose or from such a sacrificial heart, but we can always ask God to give us eyes to see where we can serve to meet heartfelt needs—both within our families and outside our homes. When our children ask why we serve, we can genuinely say, "Because they need what we need: daily bread—both

the nourishing kind and the spiritual kind." Jesus said to his disciples, "Whatever you did for one of the least of these brothers and sisters of mine, you did for me" (Matthew 25:40, NIV).

When you feed a family that isn't your own, you are serving goodness! When you love and provide for a child who is not your own, you are doing so while looking straight into the eyes of Jesus. He has received your gifts for his children and is using them to bless others. Your giving hasn't gone unrecognized. In fact, it's likely to be imitated by your children and grandchildren because they first saw it in you.

You are . . .

a servant

Mom, it's no surprise to me that you are a true servant in our family. Your decisions to serve me one day at a time have been a blessing in my life. Thank you for always noticing what I need and serving me with your words and actions. You do it out of your heart to love me, and I accept it with sincere gratefulness. I hope you know the impact you've had on my life. Thank you for your steward-ship and your commitment to my growth!

Life Together with You

Above all, clothe yourselves with love, which binds us all together in perfect harmony.

COLOSSIANS 3:14

Some of the hardest days are when we have to say good-bye to our children at the school bus, at the college dorm, before dropping them off at the airport, or when they leave the house to move out on their own.

Whether you have experienced these days yet or not, you know you will, and you cherish the time you have together with your child while you can. The word *together* closely resembles the words *to gather*, and don't we love time gathered with our kids? If your children are close with their siblings, you see this togetherness taking place on many levels—and that's a beautiful thing. But no one can take your place. After all, you are the one who has gathered moments with them from birth.

When our children are young, we may feel that the togetherness is constant. They seem to have a tracking device on us! Sometimes we're not even able to break free to get dressed for the day. And while we love their precious little faces peering into our bathroom, we would also like "just a moment."

But it's when those moments fade that we wish our children would come peering back into our rooms to check on us, ask us to play, or say with a toast-crusted, jelly-smeared face, "Are you ready?" . . . meaning they have the next game for you, the next stuffed animal you need to perform surgery on, or the next book to read.

Togetherness sure does do a lot of gathering of hearts, doesn't it? The Bible says that we are to "encourage each other and build each other up" (1 Thessalonians 5:11). Sometimes we're distracted in our togetherness. But if we want to bless our children, we can show them our affection and give them our time—especially by calling on God together. These are such special moments. Whether in seasons of health and joy or sickness and routine problems, we learn utter dependence on God as we pray and read the Bible together. In doing so, we form a foundation for our families that builds connections and expresses love, bridging our hearts together.

you are . . .

connected

Mom, you and I are connected in such a way that no one else can take the place of you. Our moments together mean so much to me, whether we are outdoors, sharing a favorite memory, or forging a new talent we both want to explore. From birth you have stayed with me, and our bond is a delight I will hold on to for a lifetime. When you choose me, our connection makes the rest of my day better!

Where You Go

I promise you what I promised Moses: "Wherever you set foot, you will be on land I have given you."

JOSHUA 1:3

"Come on. It's safe. You can do it!" How many times have we said this to our children, coaxing them toward us when they're not sure of their steps or when we see them hesitate to try new skills? We want to remind our kids that they can trust us, to assure them we know where they can safely plant their feet. If only they could see what we've grown to see with our mature eyes, from years of deciding which rocks to step over and which are smooth enough for passage.

After Moses led the Israelites out of Egypt and into a desert on their way to the land that God had promised them, things didn't go so well. The Israelites complained and didn't want to take another step. They even thought they had been better off in slavery. So Moses continually looked up to God, crying out for guidance, and he remained protected by God as he led the men, women, and children forward.

What was it that got them through? Their eyes had to focus not on their steps but on what God had promised them. And isn't the same true for us? Moses must have thought, *Come on, children of Israel—stop fretting. You can do this! You just need to trust God and put your feet where your faith is.*

When God appointed Joshua as the new leader of the Israelites, God reminded him that wherever he set foot, it would be on land that God had given him. It didn't require proof of ownership, a move-in date, or a second opinion. In fact, since God had provided the area in which they were to conquer and dwell, they could count on it. And the steps to get there would be accounted for, as only he could provide the plan, the place, and the route.

There are days when we feel like we must have taken the wrong route. We question our own steps. *Why did I go this way? Am I at the right job? Is that my child saying or doing that?* What we need is a good teaspoonful of promise to lead our way ahead. Rather than frantically trying to run ahead of God, we must keep in pace with him, watching for his cues on where we're to go. Just as we know what awaits our children as we encourage them to take the next step, God knows what's ahead for us, and we can trust him to light our path.

You are . . .

protected

Mom, your prayers mean so much to me, and I pray for you as well. I pray that God will guide you and direct your steps. You are protected, and you live the life he has for you as you walk with him. There may be storms around you, but they don't have to be inside you. You are strong in our family, and I am thankful for the safe haven God provides when we need him most. Isn't it beautiful to look at the ground beneath us and think about moving where God has given us the ability to go? Especially in uncertain times. If we take hold of this promise, we can have a new perspective and walk in strength!

Finding Space

He himself gives life and breath to everything, and he satisfies every need.

ACTS 17:25

Have you ever noticed how when you make more space in a closet or room that it lets some light in? Space creates an openness so you can actually see what you have. How about when you make more room in your heart for the child God has given you to raise? Sometimes you can't see what they need until then. Other times you need to create playful space where you have moments to connect. Or perhaps you need mental space to reset your thoughts before initiating a conversation that will bring light and understanding to your relationship.

Finding this space can sometimes feel like another item on the to-do list. But taking care of what's in your heart so that you can fully understand theirs is important. Sometimes we cling to our kids, desiring to be present with them so much that we don't allow ourselves to pause, back up, or move to the side so that we can see their needs and ours.

Being intentional to sort through your stuff often takes work, doesn't it? But making that space says to your child, "You're so important that I'm going to take some time and breathe right now so that I can offer you my all." It allows you to take care of you and get what you need before you try to parent. You are not selfish when you attend an exercise class to keep your body active, or spend time reading or listening to something that inspires you, or engage

in a creative outlet. Even when you allow time to lighten your load by sorting through a closet, you are making a way to offer your whole self to the one you are parenting. Having margin allows you to parent well.

How are you finding space? A long bubble bath has been known to bring glorious alone time, or a long walk around the block can provide relaxation and fill your lungs with fresh air so that when you're called upon, you have some reservoir. You can better respond to your child, teen, or young adult from a place of having cared for your own soul, which allows you to properly see theirs. Mom, you are so deserving of care!

you can . . .

breathe

Mom, I pray you can breathe in deeply to be able to see your role as a worthy one and take time for you. The higher you go in reaching new heights, the more difficult breathing becomes—just like a rise in elevation. But I see you breathing in the goodness of God and of life, even in the uphill climbs. May you find space in your days to fill them with what helps you come alive. I love you, Mom!

Braving Setbacks

*If you keep quiet at a time like this,
deliverance and relief for the Jews will
arise from some other place. . . . Who
knows if perhaps you were made queen
for just such a time as this?*

ESTHER 4:14

Many of us moms don't think about physically saving our family. We focus on saving dinner, saving memories our kids have gifted us, or saving what's left of their growing-up years.

Esther in the Bible hadn't thought about saving her family either—that is, until after she had married King Xerxes, who, without knowing Esther's Jewish nationality, decreed that the Jews should be destroyed. God had put Esther in a powerful place at a powerful time to protect her people from losing their lives. She was willing to risk her life for the Jews and marched forward through the doors the Lord had opened for her. She likely couldn't envision what would unfold, but she knew she had to keep going. She couldn't give up or let down her people.

Although our situations are very different from Esther's, on the days when our own families face crises and must move forward from difficulties, we can think back to the strength Esther had to keep going and know that God will not leave us in a desolate place. Just like Esther, God has given us strength to bravely resist defeat and use our positions as women, as moms, to help move our families forward in faith.

Do we rise up for our families when we need to? When setbacks come, do we grow through them or get angry in them? How do we handle the promptings in us to protect what we know is right for our families? We must take our responsibilities to heart. Esther didn't have her mother to teach her what to do. But she had something that we all can have—the strength of God in her to be noticed for such a time as this.

Will you stand up when it's time? Do you see the faces of your people and think, *I want to do everything I can for them*? You're in good company with Esther. She knew what it meant to go out on a limb, trust God, and say and do what was necessary. And that is also one of the best traits about moms. We have that instinctual knowing of what to do and say, and we are greatly valued for it!

You are . . .

strong

Mom, Queen Esther was able to read a situation and depend on God to come through for her. The boldness and inner strength he gave her allowed her the king's ear and favor. I see the same determination in you. You have a strength that I have leaned on and seen take root in our family. Thank you for always trusting in God and pushing forward even in difficult situations. Watching you brave setbacks has taught me that I can do the same. You are strong in the Lord!

Listening In

*Since we know he hears us when we
make our requests, we also know that
he will give us what we ask for.*

1 JOHN 5:15

How many of us can think back to the times we have spoken the words *Are you listening?* to our children to make sure they were hearing us? Sometimes we even repeat ourselves so we know we have their full attention. But when the situation is in reverse and our children ask, "Did you hear me?" while we go through the motions of pretending to listen, we show them that we aren't exactly following along. It turns out our kids aren't the only ones who might have a hard time listening.

What happens when we feel unheard? It produces frustration. We think that if we don't get an answer right away from our children, family members, or God, they must not be hearing us. So we put our questions on repeat, and our frustration mounts.

But we can know for sure that God hears us. He tells us in his Word that whatever we ask of him we know we will have. Peace in our hearts—check. Patience with others, including our children—yep. Reassurance of his love—you bet. We can ask him for many things, including better relationships and listening ears to hear and love each other well.

How well do we listen to our children and to God? Instead of listening with our mouths open—ready to speak— we listen with our ears and to the voice of the Spirit within us. By doing so, we will hear what we need to hear and show our love and care.

Here's a prayer that can help put us on the path to good listening:

God, today I want to lean in and listen to you more than I have before. I realize that you have important things to tell me, and I've not always been patient to listen or give you my full attention. What do you want to say that I haven't heard well before? Help me to give you my love and attention, and help me to do the same for my children by listening to them. Amen.

you are . . .

a listener

Mom, thank you for being a good listener to me. Your gift of attention gives me what I need to confidently come to you. It also shows me that I can bring my cares and questions to God, knowing he desires to listen. I want to model your example and be a better listener so that I can honor and respect your heart and what you want to share with me. I love you, Mom!

Praying for Each Other

Why am I so honored, that the mother of my Lord should visit me? When I heard your greeting, the baby in my womb jumped for joy. You are blessed because you believed that the Lord would do what he said.

LUKE 1:43-45

Moms can find a great gift in praying with each other for their children. Knowing that someone cares enough to pray for you through your pregnancy or as you raise your child is a treasure beyond compare.

Can you imagine how Elizabeth and Mary must have prayed for each other and smiled and laughed—each still in shock that they were actually carrying a child? The Bible tells us that Elizabeth was up in years, and Mary was a young virgin whom the Holy Spirit gifted the Lord Jesus to. But these women built their faith up through prayer and acknowledged what God was doing in them and through them, even in their surprise.

The story goes like this: After Mary heard from the angel that she was going to conceive, she went to visit Elizabeth, who was in her sixth month of pregnancy. The Bible says, "At the sound of Mary's greeting, Elizabeth's child leaped within her, and Elizabeth was filled with the Holy Spirit. Elizabeth gave a glad cry and exclaimed to Mary, 'God has blessed you above all women, and your child is blessed'" (Luke 1:41-42).

Even in the surprise of their situations, these women delighted. And they recognized that they were each blessed with a child, speaking that blessing aloud.

How wonderful it is when moms encourage and pray with each other for their children, not just when they are little but also as they grow—and as we grow with them.

We can gain strength for whatever situation we are in when we know someone else is there with us. A community of moms and grandmothers is valuable to the lives of our children as well—giving them a strong support system of love and care.

May you know how much your prayers for other moms and children mean to them and what your spiritual investment can bring back to your heart as well—a communion of hearts encircling each other in prayer. Imagine building a fortified wall of protection as you ask for wisdom to lead as a parent or grandparent and for your children to realize who God made them to be as they hear you pray.

Mom, thank you for praying for me. When you pray with another mom for my well-being and the direction I am going in life, I know that you have given me to God and aren't holding on to me too tightly. I'm reminded of Matthew 18:19-20: "If two of you agree here on earth concerning anything you ask, my Father in heaven will do it for you. For where two or three gather together as my followers, I am there among them." So I'm grateful. I believe that prayers between a mom and a child are very special to the Lord as well, showing their covenant with him. What a joy it is knowing he hears and honors our prayers for each other!

Putting Your Needs over Mine

Live a life filled with love, following the example of Christ. He loved us and offered himself as a sacrifice for us, a pleasing aroma to God.

EPHESIANS 5:2

As parents, there's something about seeing our children having their needs met that causes us to want to sacrifice our own needs much of the time. New pairs of warm and sturdy boots go to our children when our own are worn out, or our time in the evenings goes to helping them finish school projects—when what we really need is rest.

But God sees these selfless acts in alignment with his heart for us. He knows exactly what we need, and he sent his Son, Jesus, to take care of those needs. He put our needs over his own to show that though the world was hopeless, his Son was the answer. While many mocked and ridiculed Jesus, he knew that by sacrificing his life, many would be saved and that his Father would be glorified. Jesus showed us that our greatest need is to know our good and loving Father, who doesn't just limit our prayer requests, but holds them all in his steady hands.

As moms, needs can become objects of weight on us, can't they? *I need to get dinner on the table. My daughter needs that medication. My son doesn't need that school form but this one.* We feel as if our children are doling out needs left and right. But when we're run down, we can ask God for guidance. We can bring our children into prayer with us to see how he'll provide. Even when answers don't come in the packages we'd like them to, we know that God has already lovingly met our needs. Jesus said, "Love each other in the same way I have loved you. There is no greater love than to lay down one's life for one's friends" (John 15:12-13).

If we made a list of everything our moms gave us, often sacrificially, it might resemble a Christmas list. We are fortunate to have moms on this earth who are willing to look their children in the eyes and tell them that they are worth loving, worth sacrificing for, and that they are seen and heard. Even more, we are blessed to have a heavenly Father who provides so graciously for us so our every need is met.

you are . . .

sacrificial

Thank you, Mom, for being sacrificial so that I didn't have to go without. Your steadfast love and the ways you show me that I'm worth it dig deep into my soul. I know I wouldn't be who I am without your example. You've shown me through prayer how God meets my every need. I want to be of service to you, too, and pray for your needs. I love you, Mom!

Tree of Life-Giving Words

The Holy Spirit produces this kind of fruit in our lives: love, joy, peace, patience, kindness, goodness, faithfulness, gentleness, and self-control.

GALATIANS 5:22-23

Some of the most memorable moments with your child are not the grand, planned-out ones but the ones that sneak up on you. The loving way you hold your toddler when they scrape their knee or comfort your grown child when they are having a tough week.

There is a special place for a mom who picks the right fruit to share with her child. She has this fruit in her tree of life-giving words. Kindness is on her lips along with good-ness, faithfulness, and self-control. She knows what will encourage her child at the right moment.

Can you picture living in a desert where you must refill your water jugs daily? Can you picture the dust and heat and the way your mouth literally comes to life when you take a drink of cool, life-giving water?

When the woman at the well, as she is known in the Bible, went to get her fill, something more than water soothed her—the unexpected words of Jesus. He extended kindness to her, a woman with a reputation. Rather than calling her character into question, Jesus simply told her there was living water that would quench her thirst for life.

Can you imagine the thoughtful words he must have used that brought compassion to her when she may have expected rebuke? I bet while she ran home, spilling what-ever water she had collected, she also spilled the words of kindness that Jesus spoke over her to her family and friends.

When you speak kindness over your child, you are giving them a lifeline to discover more of God. Your thoughtfulness can actually lead them to be honest and say, "It was me, Mom. I did it" or "I messed up, but you're still being nice to me. How come?" And in those moments, you are pouring some living water into their cup—the cup they hold out for others to fill. Except we aren't able to fill it like he can, are we?

If you have a short supply of kindness, know that it's not something that can be mustered up—but it is something you can ask Jesus for. Let him fill your cup before you try to fill the cup of the child looking back at you.

Kindness releases honesty, empathy, and care. Giving your loved one this gift brings them back to you when they need you most. What thoughtfulness do you want to deliver today?

you are . . .

kind

Mom, thank you for the many times you have been so kind to me. Your kindness is the fruit of God's work in your life, and it has blessed me. Thank you for being so loving and thoughtful, even when I've wronged you or I didn't deserve it. Your words have been life-giving to me. I love you, Mom!

Bringing Loose Ends Together

*God will generously provide all you need.
Then you will always have everything you
need and plenty left over to share with others.*

2 CORINTHIANS 9:8

You heroically come through with the costume. You pack lunches with precision and speed. You wrap presents for your child to bring to birthday parties, and you provide for their own party to such a Herculean degree that you are completely worn out afterward.

Yes, moms are masters at bringing loose ends together for just about everything that passes through their hands. And even as your child ages, your fingers continue to dance—through piles of papers until you find the missing homework assignment and through department store racks as you help find the perfect dress or suit for the dance.

We moms are always using our skills to provide for our children's needs. Often this requires thinking ahead, staying on top of day-to-day demands, and having a giant rope to lasso all the things together on cue. Your child becomes more aware of your connect-the-dot movements as they get older. They develop the ability to see you as someone who not only makes them clean their room but also makes big efforts to sustain their success.

They begin saying thank you because they recognize that you're someone who not only takes care of their needs but is also the source of what meeting those needs brings: trust, thankfulness, relief, gratitude, and appreciation for what they couldn't see. We are training our kids to have greater character qualities.

But where do moms get the ability to handle all these things? By turning to God, our ultimate Provider, and praying that the homework paper will turn up or that we'll have the energy needed to do everything in a day. By slowing down and praying, we can show our young people there is One who helps us in all of life, One who promises to generously give us everything we need.

Moms know that our children see not just our actions but also our attitudes. And a prayerful posture is something they will carry with them into adulthood. When you leap to take care of what you can but also turn to God to pull all the pieces together, that is a wonderful example for your child to experience. They will learn that God knows our needs and desires to take care of them.

you are . . .

a provider

Mom, I'm deeply grateful that you are a wonderful provider. I'm sure it didn't always feel like you could master what I needed from you, and it probably wasn't easy or timely when I asked you to pull things together for me. Thank you for doing it anyway—and for doing it with heart. I have learned from you how to do many things, but best of all I've learned to lean on God and trust him to provide.

Interested in My Well-Being

God is not unjust. He will not forget how hard you have worked for him and how you have shown your love to him by caring for other believers, as you still do.

HEBREWS 6:10

Cares for others. It's one of the best qualities we can notice about each other, isn't it? Can you think back to your grade school days when report cards came out and there were handwritten notes on them from the teacher? If your card said, "She cares for others," it might have made up for any grades that weren't quite what your parents were expecting. The glowing character review still made them proud.

Caring for others is a remarkable quality that matters not only in the days of sharing desks, pencils, and crayons, but also in the days of learning to be a mom who loves diligently. Caring is a facet of loving. How do you care for your child?

When you put aside what you had hoped to accomplish for the day to help your child put the finishing touches on the heartfelt craft they made for a friend, you are showing your child you care. When you wash another load of laundry so they can have the shirt they want to wear to school or when you wake up early to quiz them before a test, you are stepping in as someone who shows that their interests are important to you. And when you radiate God's love and care to them day in and day out, you are glorifying your Father in heaven.

We can never outgive God. He is so generous! And what a wonderful habit you are building when you are generous with all you put your hands to. Your children can see and reflect the ways you care for others by serving them with your gifts. What a gracious life principle for your legacy to future generations.

Moms and the ones they love can refresh one another and be thoughtful in their love simply because it's the best choice to make each day. Moms don't just offer a hand; they also open up their caring arms.

you are . . .

caring

Mom, you have consistently shown me how you are interested in my well-being. Thank you for caring for me always. I love that you are compassionate toward me. When you compliment me or delight in what I'm doing, I come alive. You have a heart to see the best in me, and your thoughtful ways help me to notice that through you I am cared for. I can care for others because of the ways I've been cared for. I love you, Mom!

Making Memories

I remember your genuine faith, for you share the faith that first filled your grandmother Lois and your mother, Eunice. And I know that same faith continues strong in you. This is why I remind you to fan into flames the spiritual gift God gave you when I laid my hands on you. For God has not given us a spirit of fear and timidity, but of power, love, and self-discipline.

2 TIMOTHY 1:5-7

One of the heroes of faith who taught us we have God's power and love inside of us is Paul. He was writing to Timothy, whom he was mentoring, reminding him of his lineage of faith that began with his grandmother and mother—quite a legacy of women, it seems. Wouldn't we like to be known as women who pass on a strong faith to our children and grandchildren?

Some of us might not realize that our faith and spiritual gifts can help us create memories for our children and grandchildren. And while we may not always recognize our spiritual gifts, they are there! God has created us to make these memories with and for our children to draw us closer together and set our hearts on his purposes for us. When we do so, we are implanting physical and spiritual memories into their lives—the physical memories of being with them and enjoying moments that tie our hearts together, and the spiritual memories that plant seeds, share beliefs, and create a foundation of faith for them.

When we are intentional about making these kinds of memories, we give our children a lifetime of love and biblical truth to look back on. Memories are to a life what pennies are to a piggy bank; what we put in doesn't necessarily make a big difference in the moment, but as we are faithful to add more, the amount grows significantly over time.

One of the ways moms can create memories is through keeping traditions passed on from previous generations. Just as Timothy's mother and grand-mother passed their faith on, we can help build our children's faith through reading the Bible to them, singing worship songs together, and showing them the importance of specific holidays, like Christmas and Easter, through fun activities.

You probably have your own traditions that come to mind—digging out your grandmother's cookie recipe and putting ornaments on the tree each year, lighting the candles at Advent, going on an Easter egg hunt. These traditions help create the opportunities we crave as mothers: seeing our children's faces light up, starting conversations we wouldn't have otherwise had, and spending quality time together. You are knitting memories to look back on when they are grown that they, too, will be able to pass on to their children and grandchildren.

You are . . .

memorable

Mom, thank you for making memories with me. I enjoy time with you and the ways we have created lasting moments together. You have shown me how to hang on to a moment and carry it forward. You inspire me to want to create lasting memories in the future that I can share with others. Thank you for being someone who knows how to bring spontaneity and fun to the moment but who has also led me to deeper faith through the encouragement and wisdom you share. You are a memory-maker to remember!

Assurance of My Love and God's

The LORD your God is living among you.
  He is a mighty savior.
He will take delight in you with gladness.
  With his love, he will calm all your fears.
He will rejoice over you with joyful songs.

ZEPHANIAH 3:17

Have you ever told your child you loved them, only to see them react with a scrunched-up face that made you wonder whether your hair was a mess or you had something in your teeth? Their eyes met yours as if to say, "Really, you do?"

Sometimes what's underneath that uncertainty is, "I needed to hear that." And sometimes as parents we realize we needed to say that—especially after a day of yelling or arguments. You have likely heard the phrase "What's down in the well comes up in the bucket." What's inside of us will come up and out, but what will it be?

Like opening a gift with your name on it, it's a delight to see the care and thought others have for you—especially when that gift shows God's love. Zephaniah was a man who had a message for people who needed to hear it. He had some words that rang out and were cinched in the hearts of those who caught them. He connected the heart of God to the one listening, telling them that God takes delight in us, loves us, and rejoices over us. He gave assurance to those who were pressing in, wondering whether they were lovable, and his words soothed their souls.

You know how when your child cries out, your presence or touch brings calm and assurance that all will be well? It is well in God's love too. You are loved not by what title you hold or who you have been or will become, but because you are his daughter. His intended creation. You can be assured that his love for you was established through Jesus before you were even born (Ephesians 1:4). He sacrificed his life for you. And he knew that you would need to be held tight and told again and again that he loves you.

Sometimes we try to give our children what we actually need ourselves: Assurance. The freedom to be loved just as we are, like a child who doesn't need to get everything right before coming to a parent, whose unconditional love was sealed in their heart the day their child was born.

Even if you have never fully experienced that kind of love, you can be certain that God sings over you now, just as you sing or have sung over your own child. And when God is singing over you, you don't need to hear another voice. As you rejoice over your child, know that your Father is rejoicing over you.

you are ...

loved

Mom, you have raised me to love and know love, and for that I'm grateful. We may feel as though we have fallen short at times, but I want you to know that God's love is enough for both of us. His perfect love fills in where we need it to, and he gives us assurance of his love by rejoicing over us. When you need a reassuring word that I see you for who you are, know that I give back to you what you have always shown me—the understanding and declaration that you are loved!

A Life of No Regrets

You keep track of all my sorrows.
  You have collected all my tears in your bottle.
  You have recorded each one in your book.

My enemies will retreat when I call to you for help.
  This I know: God is on my side!

PSALM 56:8-9

Life can get so busy sometimes that we don't take advantage of opportunities we have to tell those we love how we feel; or life can be so stressful that we say harmful things in the heat of the moment. We might be in tears over the things we wish we had said, or perhaps we are weighed down by regret because of what we *did* say. People may tell us that time will heal our hurts or that we just need to hold it together, but we know that we can't overlook how we feel.

Sometimes the best thing we can do is bring our regrets before God and lean on him for understanding. He sees our tears, wipes them away, and records them. He doesn't overlook our emotions. He is compassionate when we hurt from disappointment and when we grieve loss and change. It helps to know that he always listens and gives us a way back to the words we have been searching for to share with others.

And through him, we can start where we are today. We can let go of what we wish we had done differently or what we can't change. We can go to our mom or child and recall the times when we felt closer, telling them, "I appreciate you and admire you for who you are. I want to remind you that the best things between us remain, and no matter where we are, you are close in my mind and heart. Whatever words we have let slip by, we can bring them back and forge a new path today. You are worth the words I want to give you."

When we give God our regrets, we are opening doors that may have been held shut before. We are taking a stance of forgiveness and healing. We are operating without anything standing in the way so that we may seal our relationship with our mom or child and begin anew.

Sealing and healing our hearts is God's expertise. He invented relationships, repairs relationships, and gives us words that heal. When we wish we could take back what we or a loved one said, our part is to go to him and ask for healing that can only come from him. And in doing so, we will have no regrets.

You are . . .

unforgettable

Mom, at times our words have been stuck hanging in the past, somewhere between good intentions and "I should have said . . ." But no matter what has been left unsaid, I want you to know how thankful I am for the role you have played in my life. You are unforgettable in how you have loved me and forgiven me time and again. I am grateful for what we've learned from each other and from God and how compassion has always renewed our course. Your love is like a rainbow spreading out over my life! I love you, Mom!

Blessing Giver

The LORD bless you and keep you;
the LORD make his face to shine upon
you and be gracious to you;
the LORD lift up his countenance upon
you and give you peace.

NUMBERS 6:24-26, ESV

There are times when we want to offer a special blessing to someone for who they are in our lives. And for moms, this is especially true because they are life bearers. Moms pour out so much of themselves for their children and don't always get filled back up—but they do it gladly and cheerfully. Dear mom, you are a blessing giver. And it's your turn to have blessings of love, delight, and joy heaped on you. May God show his faithfulness to you as he blesses you with gifts from above.

God's face shining down on you and the warmth of his love for you affirms who you are in his eyes. Whether you feel like you have done a good job raising your child or whether you don't feel as close to your child as you would like, may you know that the God of all creation looks upon you as someone he loves and delights in very much. Genesis 1:27-28, 31 says, "God created human beings in his own image. . . . Male and female he created them. Then God blessed them and said, 'Be fruitful and multiply. Fill the earth and govern it. . . . Then God looked over all he had made, and he saw that it was very good!"

We know that God doesn't look back on anything he has made with anything other than marvel. And he says, "You are very good." We can say those words over ourselves and our children because his words are true. If the God of the universe loves us, how can we not think the best of ourselves?

Mom, you have given so many blessings over your lifetime. May you receive this blessing over you:

May God bless you beyond your imagination. May he keep you close and cover you with his divine protection and guidance each day of your life. May he produce a sparkle in your eyes and a heart for his glory that gives you grace for every challenge you encounter. May he bring you peace as you set your mind on the tasks and responsibility of loving your child even in their shortcomings—a mirror of how much God loves you. May the blessings God gives you last beyond your lifetime!

you are . . .

a blessing

I love you, Mom. You have blessed me in so many ways, and today I want to bless you. Through all that we have experienced as a family and all that we will continue to face together, I ask God to bestow his love and grace upon you. Thank you for the way you have delighted in me and led me in love. May God's blessings over you carry on for generations to come.

A space for Mom
to reflect